THE SCOTTISH HIGHLANDS

PHOTOGRAPHS BY

COLIN BAXTER

THE SCOTTISH HIGHLANDS

The Scottish Highlands reach from the outer fringes of the sprawling metropolis of Glasgow in the south to the northernmost tip of the British mainland at Duncansby Head. They form a rugged and remote landscape, majestic and magical in equal measure.

Mighty snow-capped mountain peaks rise above wraiths of mist to create a dark and mysterious world inhabited by creatures with strange-sounding names, such as Schiehallion, Sgùrr na Ciste Duibhe, Stob Coir' an Albannaich and Stùc a' Chroin. Deep, sinuous lochs interplay with these high mountain ranges, most famously Loch Lomond and Loch Ness, in whose dark depths lurks the legendary monster.

Nature is everywhere. Large herds of deer stalk the straths and glens, whilst silvery salmon swim and spawn in the fast-flowing rivers; overhead soar eagle and osprey, ptarmigan and grouse. Fragile plants and vestiges of Scotland's ancient Caledonian pine forest cling determinedly to the thin soils, none with more fragility than the rare alpine plants that shimmer and shiver in the sub-Arctic paradise that is the Cairngorm Mountains, the most extensive area of granite mountain massif in the British Isles.

Human settlement is sparse in this largely natural world. It was not always thus. In centuries gone by, before the infamous Highland Clearances of the early 19th century, the straths and glens teemed with thousands of people, trying their best to tame nature. But nature was always going to prevail. The landlords hastened the end, inducing their tenants to leave the land of their forebears for the mines and factories, or to emigrate to distant lands such as Canada and Australia, leaving their abandoned crofts to the sheep and the stag.

But although the landlords could take the man out of the mountains, they could not take the mountains out of the man. The 'mist-covered mountains of home' have lived on in the collective memory, so that today the Scottish Highlands are deeply embedded in the Scottish psyche.

BEN VENUE & LOCH KATRINE, Trossachs, Stirlingshire (left), and looking south across the loch (above) – this is 'Rob Roy' MacGregor country, for the famous outlaw, rebel and cattle dealer was born here at Loch Katrine in 1671.

LOCH LOMOND, Dunbartonshire (above), looking towards Beinn Ime, with Ben Lui and Ben Cruachan in the distance, and BEN LOMOND (right) seen from the west across Loch Lomond – the largest expanse of fresh water in Britain.

INVERARAY CASTLE, Loch Fyne, Argyll, from the air (right) – the castellated Gothic mansion was built c1750 as the new Highland seat of the Campbells, Dukes of Argyll. Argyllshire had been 'Campbells' Kingdom' since the 14th century.

LOCH FYNE, Argyll, from the south (left) – the neat town of Inveraray, Argyll's first royal burgh in 1648, was rebuilt in tandem with the castle, and provides a point of light amidst the gathering clouds above Glen Fyne.

KILCHURN CASTLE, Loch Awe, with Ben A'Chleibh and Ben Lui beyond (left) – Sir Colin Campbell, Lord of Glenorchy, a kinsman of the Campbell Earls of Argyll, built the formidable stronghold in the 15th century.

LOCH AWE, Argyll, looking west from near the north end of the loch (right) – the Campbell lords of Argyll had a sizeable fleet of galleys on the loch in the Middle Ages, as well as Innischonnel Castle on an island near the south shore, now a ruin.

CASTLE STALKER, Argyll – built on Loch Linnhe by the Stewarts of Appin in the 16th century.

LOCH SUNART, Lochaber (left) – looking north towards the snow-capped peak of Beinn Resipol.

OBAN HARBOUR, Argyll – this attractive seaport serves as the 'gateway' to the Hebrides.

LOCH CRERAN, Argyll (right) with the two peaks of BEINN SGURLAIRD beyond.

BIDEAN NAM BIAN, Glencoe, (right) seen from across Loch Achtriochtan – it is said that in a cave hereabouts, Ossian, the only human to enter the paradise of Tir-an-Og, the 'Land of Youth', and return alive, met with St Patrick of Ireland.

'THE THREE SISTERS', Glencoe, (left) – the 'sisters', named Beinn Fhada, Gearr Aonach and Aonach Dubh, loom high above the Pass of Glencoe. Here, in February 1692, the Clan MacDonald of Glencoe were murdered in their sleep by the guests who had accepted their hopitality for 12 days, in the infamous 'Massacre of Glencoe'.

THE GLENFINNAN MONUMENT & LOCH SHIEL, Lochaber (left) – the monument, erected in 1815, marks the spot where, on 19 August 1745, Bonnie Prince Charlie raised his father's royal standard to begin the '45 Jacobite Rising.

GLENFINNAN VIADUCT, Lochaber (right) – one of the highlights of the West Highland Line, the 21-arched viaduct links Fort William with the port of Mallaig. In summer, a popular Jacobite steam train is an added attraction to the service.

THE MORAR COASTLINE, Lochaber – located along the 'Road to the Isles' between Arisaig and Mallaig, the area has distinctive white sandy beaches framed by rocky outcrops. The views to the west are impressive and take in the 'Small Isles' of Rum, Eigg and Muck.

BLACK MOUNT, Rannoch Moor – a wild landscape to the south of Glencoe.

BEN NEVIS across Loch Eil (right) – at 4408 ft (1344 m), the highest mountain in Britain.

LOCH TAY, Perthshire, (left) and BEN CHALLUM & GLEN LOCHY, Stirlingshire (above).

GLEN LYON, Perthshire (above and right) – one of the most beautiful Highland glens.

LOCH TUMMEL & SCHIEHALLION from 'QUEEN'S VIEW', Perthshire.

BLAIR CASTLE, Perthshire (left) – has served as the chief seat of the Dukes of Atholl for centuries.

CREAG MEAGAIDH, Central Highlands – a National Nature Reserve renowned for its native woodland of birch, alder, rowan, willow and oak. The ice-carved rock crags are popular with climbers in winter.

LOCH LAGGAN, Badenoch – the waters power an aluminium works in Fort William.

THE CAIRNGORMS from near Aviemore (above), and LOCH INSH, Strathspey (right).

BALMORAL CASTLE & RIVER DEE, Royal Deeside. The Castle is the Highland home of the royal family.

BRAES OF ABERNETHY, Cairngorms – foothills on the northern side of the Cairngorm Mountains.

CARRBRIDGE, Strathspey – built in 1717 to carry pedestrians and horses over the River Dulnain, and also hearses heading for the kirkyard at Duthil; hence its nickname 'Coffin Bridge'. The parapets were washed away in the floods of 1829.

RUTHVEN BARRACKS, Strathspey (above) and STRATHSPEY, looking south-west from near Coylumbridge (right) – the barracks were built after the Jacobite Rising of 1715 to help patrol the Strath. General Wade added the stables (foreground) in 1734.

URQUHART CASTLE & LOCH NESS – the mighty castle stood sentinel beside the loch for over 500 years, until its destruction following the Jacobite Rising of 1689. At around 23 miles long, Loch Ness is one of three lochs that helps form *Glen Mòr* 'the Great Glen'.

INVERNESS & THE RIVER NESS – the city is known as 'the capital of the Highlands'.

LOCH NEVIS from North Morar, Lochaber (right) – Ben Bhuidhe 'the yellow mountain' is on the left.

KNOYDART across the Sound of Sleat (left) and BEINN SGRITHEALL & LOCH HOURN (above).

THE KINTAIL MOUNTAINS, at the head of Loch Duich (above), and their dominant 'Five Sisters' (right).

EILEAN DONAN CASTLE & LOCH ALSH, WITH SKYE BEYOND (left) – the Mackenzie chiefs of Kintail built the medieval castle, and later the pretty village of DORNIE nearby (above), which stands at the confluence of Lochs Alsh, Duich and Long.

LOCH KISHORN & LOCH CARRON, Wester Ross (left) and LOCH MAREE, Wester Ross (above).

LOCH TORRIDON & LOCH SHIELDAIG, Wester Ross – Torridon has some of the most powerful landscapes in the West Highlands. The red Torridian sandstone of the region adds colour and character to the mountains, and dates from up to 1000 million years ago.

ULLAPOOL (above) and LOCH BROOM FROM ULLAPOOL PIER (right), Wester Ross. The handsome seaport was founded as a 'new town' in the late 1780s to help Highlanders profit from the herring shoals. In early summer, Loch Broom would have been crammed with fishing boats.

LOCH KANAIRD, Wester Ross (left) and STAC POLLAIDH (STAC POLLY), Wester Ross (above).

The ancient landscapes of SUILVEN (above) and OLDSHOREMORE (right), Sutherland.

DUNNET BAY, Caithness – Dunnet Head is the most northerly point of mainland Britain.

DORNOCH BRIDGE & DORNOCH FIRTH (left) – with the Sutherland mountains in the distance.

BEN LOYAL & THE KYLE OF TONGUE (above) and SANDWOOD BAY, looking towards Cape Wrath (right), Sutherland – the unspoiled beauty of these northern landscapes reflects their isolaton and exposure to some of Scotland's harshest weather.

The remote landscapes of FOINAVEN and STRATH DIONARD, north-west Sutherland.

Published in Great Britain in 2008 by Colin Baxter Photography Ltd,
Grantown-on-Spey, Moray PH26 3NA, Scotland

www.colinbaxter.co.uk

Photographs © Colin Baxter 2008
Text by Chris Tabraham

A CIP Catalogue record for this book is available
from the British Library.

ISBN 978-1-84107-364-4 Printed in China

Page one photograph: HIGHLAND COW
Page two photograph: GLEN AVON and RIVER AVON, Moray
Front cover photograph: LOCHNAGAR & BALMORAL, Royal Deeside
Back cover photograph: LOCH AFFRIC, GLEN AFFRIC, West Highlands